The White Book

Gary Hope

"The White Book," by Gary Hope

ISBN 9-781-62137-637-8 (Softcover)

Library of Congress Control Number on file with publisher.

1
"Everything in moderation... including moderation."

This is the fourth book I have written. In the first three I simply told the truth, told some stories, listed some trivial information and repeated some history that some of us may have forgotten. This, however, is a biased book (my biases...since it's my book); my intention is to explain how I think about things, how I view religion, politics and the state of affairs in our world. Certainly, the quickest way to alienate people is to voice your views on religion (or politics, which to some people borders on religion), but I don't care about political correctness, nor do I care about hurting some people's feelings – maybe their feelings need to be hurt once in a while...maybe it'll wake them up. I doubt it, but heck, I may not have much longer to voice my opinions, so here they are: the good, the bad and a bunch of thoughts that'll probably make you mad.

First, I'm going to discuss religion as I see it. I'll just go ahead and alienate about 90% of you right now...no use waiting around. I'm a Christian, sometimes a decent Christian, sometimes a Christian who needs major forgiveness in his life, but still, a devoted Christian who loves Jesus Christ. I truly don't understand how anyone could not be a Christian, if you have any sense at all and any brains to think logically about our world and history. Being a

Christian, in my opinion, means loving the Lord and believing that Jesus Christ was born and died to save us from our sins. He paid a debt which we could not pay and cannot pay by dying on the cross for us. A lot of people don't believe this, bad for them, because one day we'll stand before the Lord and answer for our actions and our beliefs. The ONLY thing that will get you into heaven for eternity (zillions of years), is belief in Jesus and repentance of your sins. There is nothing else on earth you can do to enter heaven besides this...period. It doesn't matter how "good" you are, it doesn't matter how many great things you do, or how many people you help, or how much money you give to the poor – no, none of this will get you into heaven. Only your belief in Jesus will do that. I know a lot of you don't want to hear that – or believe it, but it's true.

For those of you who have doubts, tell me this: how do you explain the Bible? How do you explain how everything started? Do you REALLY think there was nothing and then nothing exploded in a "Big Bang" and then nothing somehow started replicating itself and eventually turned into fish, which then turned into dinosaurs, which then turned into monkeys, then men? Really? You do realize there is absolutely no scientific evidence of any of this happening and no trail of evolution, except in THEORY, to explain any of this. Unfortunately for the evolutionists, even their own scientists are now backtracking, saying they can find no evidence of species evolving into other species, but it simply "must have happened this way"...how else can they explain it? I'll tell you how to explain it: "In the beginning God created the heavens and the earth…" Once you get past that first sentence in the Bible, and understand it and accept it…everything else in the Bible makes perfect sense.

How do people explain Jesus? A man born over 2000 years ago who has changed the world, a man who has had more books written about Him than anyone else in history. A man who has had more paintings done of Him than anyone in history. How do you explain that? How do you explain Him dying on a cross – and die, He indeed did; the Romans were experts at killing people – then coming back to life three days later appearing to over 500 people? How do you explain that? How do you explain the twelve Apostles who witnessed these events all dying tragic, painful deaths because they wouldn't refute what they saw? Eleven of the 12 were tortured to death and any of them could have saved their own life simply by saying it wasn't true. But they couldn't say it wasn't true, because it was…they knew it, they saw it, they felt the nail prints in His hands and feet – how does anyone explain that?

As Jesus once said, "blessed is he who sees and believes, but even more blessed is he who has not seen yet still believes." Truly, there are very large groups of people who will never believe any of this, just as there are very large groups of organized religions who have twisted and turned things so crazily, it's amazing how they have convinced so many people about so many bizarre events. They have made religions of things Jesus never said or intended, they have convinced millions of people that the Bible is not entirely accurate, that their version of events are actually true...doesn't matter if there's no historical evidence of anything they say, nor any documents to substantiate their versions. No, just blindly believe them and do some good deeds and you will end up in Heaven. Hogwash! These people who lead others astray will one day have to answer for their actions before the Lord. Don't be taken in by these charlatans...The Lord gave us everything we need to know in the Bible. It's not a puzzle, nor is it a buffet line where you take what you want and leave out what you don't want. It's not golden tablets, nor undocumented histories, nor fairy tales...it is what it is: a documented history, divinely inspired, telling us all we need to know.

Now, for the Christians: we're far from PERFECT! We're forgiven, but Lord knows we've got just as many problems as anyone else. Many so-called Christians have done dastardly deeds in the Lord's name. Christians have killed those in other religious groups, they've killed each other, they've called each other names and lied about each other; history is rife with the sad plight of despicable acts done in the name of the Lord. It's sad to admit, but a lot of these actions are still occurring today. The Lord said, "Love one another." Not, kill those who are different...trust me, if you only love the people who are like you, then you will hate Heaven...if you somehow got there.

In my opinion, there are four things we should know about every person on earth. It doesn't matter how successful or unsuccessful they are, or how famous or obscure they are, or how attractive or ugly they are...everyone shares these four traits.

One, there is an essential emptiness in every person, that can only be filled by Christ. It doesn't matter how much money you have, or how famous you are; God made you with a void inside that only He can fill.

Two, people are lonely. There is a sense of loneliness in every individual.

Three, people have a sense of guilt. They may try to mask it with alcohol or drugs, or maybe even have a psychiatrist convince them it's not really there. The head of a leading mental institution once said, "I could release half of my patients if I could find a way to relieve them of their sense of guilt."

Four, people are afraid to die. Some may act brave and strut around, but when faced with death, they too are afraid, just like we all are. None of us knows how long we'll live...8 years, 38 years, 88 years, we never know what the Lord has planned for us. That is why we have to make every day count. We don't know when our day will come – when the Lord calls you home, you're going home! It won't matter how many vitamins you take, how many hours you spend in the gym, what kind of healthy foods you eat...when your number is up, it's up.

On the other hand, you will also be around until God is done with you. You won't go before your time. Doesn't really matter how healthy you are and what sort of shape you're in, you'll live to the time God has appointed for you – and worrying about it won't extend your life for one moment. Winston Churchill was a great man, but he didn't take care of himself; he drank a quart of whiskey every day and smoked up to 15 cigars daily, and he weighed nearly 300 pounds on his 5'9" body. Yet, he lived to be 90 years old. The Lord had plans for him, just as He does for you and me.

However, we aren't to be foolish either and "put the Lord to the test." Some people have misinterpreted some passages in the Bible and skewed the meanings. In one story Jesus said, "They will take up serpents; and if they drink anything deadly, it will by no means hurt them..." Some people actually test the Lord with this statement and handle snakes in worship services. That is not trusting the Lord, it is testing the Lord. The statement Jesus said means if you are a Christian, then you are indestructible until God is done with you. There is a day appointed for your death, and you really have nothing to say about when that day is.

So stop worrying about when you'll die, because you have nothing to say about it. It isn't up to you. Does that mean you can eat and drink anything you want? No, you should act responsibly and exercise and eat properly. This will improve the QUALITY of your life. But ultimately, the quantity is still up to God.

We can rest assured that we are here until God is finished with us. So make the most out of your life and every day God has given you. Wherever you are, whatever you do, be all that you can. Live life to the hilt in every situation, as long as you believe it's in the will of God.

"a good old girl"

2
You know what I got for Christmas? Fat! I got Fat!!

Politics. This subject can inflame almost any conversation--even more than religion can. And now, I'm going to do all I can to really stir up the flames. Some people actually think a political agenda or a political party can legislate morality...they really do. News flash: God isn't a Republican or a Democrat. He doesn't vote. If He did, He'd win every time. Another news flash: no one is ever elected without God's approval. Read your Bible...please read your Bible.

I've recently changed my party affiliation, I'm now the chairman of the "Non-Incumbent Party". If you are an incumbent, then I don't vote for you, doesn't matter to me which political party you're affiliated with...I ain't voting for you. I don't think our founding fathers meant for people to make careers of being politicians – if they did, then they were wrong. I think they meant for people to go to Washington, or Raleigh, or wherever; serve for the greater good for their elected term, then go back home and actually GO TO WORK! Make something of themselves, contribute to the greater good, pay their fair share of taxes, buy their own insurance, live by the same rules the rest of us live by – not mooch off the public payroll, get salaries for LIFE, even after you're no longer serving; not get free insurance (insurance by the way, that none of the rest of us can get), not get free benefits, free travel, free everything...no! Stop the free ride, go back home, go to work, pay taxes, buy your own insurance...just like every other American has to do.

I started off being a left wing Democrat back in my college days. I wasn't really political, I was just against the Vietnam War and didn't want to get drafted and sent over there. That, plus, the Democrats had much prettier girls on campus. The Republican girls were just a little too Nixony for my tastes. After graduation, I changed somewhat to being a more moderate Democrat for two reasons: first, my grandfather was a Democrat, and by God if it was good enough for Grover Cleveland Townsend, then it was good enough for me; and second, the Democrats still had the prettiest girls. I read somewhere that if you weren't a liberal when you were young, then shame on you; and if you weren't a conservative when you were old, then twice the shame on you...I think there's a lot to that.

As I grew older (not wiser, just older), I evolved into a middle of the road sort of guy and started to realize that both parties were quickly filling up with weirdos and wackos. Although I still voted for Democrats, they were increasingly trying my patience with their outlandish platforms. Several elections, I did not vote for the Democratic candidate, nor did I vote for the Republican candidate. I either chose the third party loser, or more often than not, my own write in candidate.

This has now evolved into my new party, the" Non-Incumbent Common Sense Party". It has no affiliations and no members and no pretty girls...but it makes me feel good not to vote for any of those lazy, slothful career politicians who just want to mooch off my hard earned tax dollars. I'm equally disgusted with both Democrats and Republicans; some of the things they say and believe in is just absurd. Seemingly, the Democratic platform consists solely of appeasing the gay, lesbian, transgender community (all 1.7% of them) at the expense of what the other 98.3% of Americans want. Their second concern seems to be to fund any and all people who don't want to work...to give them checks every week for not working, give them free food, free insurance and a free ride for their entire lives. Sounds like a good deal if your goal in life is be a worthless, mooching bum. The Democrats also want to allow any Hispanic person, or hundreds of thousands of persons, to enter our country illegally, then give them checks every week, and food and insurance and shelter, and a free education just because they were industrious enough to cross our borders illegally, without getting caught. In my opinion, this is outright and blatant racism! I guarantee you if my ancestors from Ireland tried to enter this country illegally, then tried to get free food, free insurance, free schooling and free everything, they'd throw them back in the ocean where they came from.

And Republicans...sometimes I wonder how they can even sleep at night. One thing I give them credit for is they don't try to hide who they are: rich, privileged socialites who want to take care of themselves and their country club friends, while stomping on the downtrodden masses who can't help themselves and actually need some government help simply to survive. I'll stop there, this hole is deep enough as is.

I feel I should address the whole homosexual, gay, lesbian, whatever issue now. First, let me simply state that as a Christian I believe homosexuality is a sin – it's not my definition, it's the Lord God's definition. If you have a problem with it being labeled a sin, then you need to argue with God, not me. However, cheating, adultery, fornication, lying, stealing, and other things are also sins – none greater or less than homosexuality. In God's eyes, a sin is a sin. And, here's the kicker—we're ALL tempted by sin. We all have desires we know are wrong, we all want to do things we know are wrong, we all give into these temptations from time to time. But, here's the good news: Jesus tells us we'll NEVER be tempted more than we can handle. We will always be able to walk away from temptation (or better yet, to run away), if we so desire. We face temptations every day, in many different forms; I even think some people are born with pre-dispositions to sins...such as alcoholism, or addictions, or even homosexuality. That doesn't mean we have to cave into these temptations...we are to fight them, to walk away from them, to repeatedly pray to the Lord for help and seek His refuge, not to give in to human temptations. This is where the gay community is trying to convince our nation that it's okay to be gay.

They say "we were born this way". Maybe so, maybe others were born with the genes towards alcoholism and addictions...that doesn't mean it's okay to give into these vices and ruin your lives. No! You fight them, you walk away from them, you seek help, you pray – if all else fails, you pray ceaselessly...that's what we're taught. Keep praying and your prayers will be answered.

The Bible says to love all people without judgment and treating gays any differently would also be a sin. I have several friends who are admittedly gay and lesbian, and I have several relatives as well. I love them as I love everyone else. I love those who lie and cheat and steal and commit all sorts of sins – because I'm one of them – we all are. We all sin and fall short of the glory of God. We all need Him, some of us more than others. Don't let Hollywood or some popular celebrities convince you otherwise. Be strong in your faith, stand up for what you believe in and what is right in the Lord's eyes...your rewards will be in heaven – guaranteed. Just because a court rules that it's legal for gays to marry doesn't make it right in God's eyes. It's still a sin, regardless of what any court rules. Many years ago, courts ruled Black people could not vote, that wasn't right. The courts ruled women couldn't vote, that wasn't right. They ruled Blacks could not use the same facilities as whites, that wasn't right either. At one time in our history the courts ruled that Americans could not drink alcohol. These are just a few of the examples of how our courts can really screw things up...why? Because the courts are made up of human beings and lawyers – need I say more? Always rely on God's laws; if there's ever any question if you should follow God's lead or man's lead, I hope you will choose wisely and make the right decision.

"Beauties"

3

"Sometimes it's fun being me."

My wife and I went to see Paul McCartney in concert last week (Oct. 30, 2014). Simply stated, he was AMAZING! The guy is 72 years old and he absolutely sang his butt off and rocked the sold out coliseum for nearly three hours. Sometimes, his other band members would go off stage and rest and get something to drink while Paul stayed onstage and sang acoustic guitar ballads like "Blackbird" or "Yesterday". He never left the stage and I never saw him get anything to drink either – I don't know how he did it. He came back for 3 encores, finally closing the concert with the song from Abbey Road, "The End". He played the bass, of course, but he also played acoustic guitar, lead guitar (with a rousing solo in tribute to Jimi Hendrix), piano, organ and ukulele (in tribute to George). He had over 22,000 people screaming and singing with delight. Not only were a lot of the crowd around my age, but there were people of all ages there…his appeal is universal and ageless. I mean the guy was best friends and wrote songs with John Lennon.

John is one of my heroes, and I used to think a cut above the other Beatles…I was wrong. Oh, don't misunderstand – John was special, but they all were – still are. It just took me longer to understand that. This was my fourth time seeing Paul in concert, and I would have to say, it was the best of the four. I saw him first way back in the early '70's when he was touring with "Wings", which included his wife Linda. Back then, he didn't play any Beatles songs, only his solo stuff and Wings material – which was okay, but we didn't kid ourselves. We wanted to hear the Beatles stuff – timeless, ageless songs that people of all ages still sing along to 50 years later.

Paul was criticized quite often for allowing Linda to be in his band (she was not a natural musician), but I totally understand it. Paul loved his wife and wanted her with him and involved in his life all the time – I get it. I admire him for being faithful to his wife and raising several successful, well-adjusted children, while not falling into the temptations of the rock & roll lifestyle that so many of his peers fell into over the years. All you need to do is listen to the lyrics of a simple little song Paul wrote for Linda that expressed how he felt:

"Who knows how long I've loved you?

You know I love you still,

will I wait a lonely lifetime,

if you want me to I will.

Love you forever and forever,

love you with all my heart;

love you whenever we're together,

love you when we're apart.

And when at last I find you,

our song will fill the air,

sing it loud so I can hear you;

make it easy to be near you,

oh, the things you do endear you to me ,

oh, you know I will......I will."

So simple, so loving, so telling...they stayed bonded together until breast cancer cruelly took Linda away from him after 29 years of marriage.

I took my wife, her sister Martha and our niece Wendy to see Paul again in Charlotte at an outdoor amphitheater in the mid 1990's. This time he sang a lot of Beatles tunes, along with Wings and solo stuff – again, it was amazing. He had the crowd in the palm of his hands and did not disappoint a single soul. I saw George Harrison in concert Friday, December 13, 1974 – how do I remember this date? Because I still have the ticket stub from that concert at the Capitol Centre in Washington, D.C. The ticket cost me $9.50 back then...worth every penny of it. I've come to love George more and more over the years and respect him musically and personally as well. Like Paul, he was faithful to his wife, Olivia, until that dreaded disease cancer took him cruelly away from us much too soon. After John found his true life's love, Yoko, he stayed with her until a madman took him from us. And Ringo was married to the beautiful Maureen until cancer took her...then he married the actress Barbara Bach, (a former Bond girl), and he's been with her ever since. Amazing to me how these four guys, adored by the world, idolized by millions and lusted after by so many young girls (including Martha Carter in her youth), all wound up all staying married to their wives for nearly their entire lives. Maybe it was something in their Liverpudlian upbringing, or maybe it was just that they really understood the meaning of "All You Need is Love...Love Is All You Need."

I took my wife, Susan, and my daughter Shelley to see Paul once again in Raleigh about 10 years ago. My daughter could not believe how good he was. She told me, "He really rocks!" Shelley...you have no idea. Thank you, Paul...thank you for being you and bringing us all these years of incredible memories and songs and experiences. If you ever decide to tour again – anywhere remotely close to here – I'll be there. "And in the end...the love you take, is equal to the love you make."

"Bloods"

4

"A politician is a fellow who will lay down your life for his country."

I have a brother-in-law named Clarence Vance Mattocks. Clarence is a lawyer, but not your stereotypical sleazy, lying, selfish, money-grubbing sort of lawyer. What other kind of lawyer is there, you might ask? The good kind…and there are some good ones; Seth and Clyde are two of the good ones. But Clarence is different. Seemingly, he's more interested in doing the right thing and in doing things right, and helping people who can't help themselves, often for no pay and quite anonymously.

He's also a Quaker. I'm not exactly sure I totally understand what being a Quaker is all about, but I think it has something to do with not caring about making a lot of money, helping the helpless, identifying every bird that flies across the North Carolina sky and being forced to root for the University of North Carolina sports teams (no matter how unpleasant that can be at times). Apparently, Quakers love to suffer.

Clarence has a relative in his family tree who was the Governor of North Carolina – twice! His middle name, Vance, stems from this heritage, and quite a heritage it is. Clarence's ancestor is named Zebulon Baird Vance and was elected Governor of North Carolina during the Civil War (or as we southerners refer to it, The Wawer Between the States). He was first elected in 1862, after initially commanding rebel forces in the battles at New Bern and at Richmond, where he was a Colonel in the Confederate Army. He was then re-elected in 1864 before being arrested on his birthday by Federal forces in May, 1865. After release, he practiced law in Charlotte and among his clients was the accused murderer Tom Dula, the subject of the folk song "Tom Dooley."

In 1876, he was elected Governor once again, and in 1879 the legislature elected him to the United States Senate, where he served until his death in 1894. He was buried in Asheville, where an impressive monument to his memory and service still graces the downtown square today. Although politics is not in Clarence's resume, servitude, loyalty, dedication and compassion are. And like Paul, Clarence has been married to the same lovely lady for about a hundred years now (maybe not that long...but close). He's reared two intelligent, beautiful daughters and made sure neither one of them went to UNC – he's wise and totally unselfish that way.

I respect Clarence and I respect his beliefs and commitment to his family, his religion and his work. I wish a lot more people could be like him. I wish I was a lot more like him – but I have to struggle with who I am and use the influences and examples of good men like Clarence and Conrad and Jerry and Dickie and Larry and Bill and Allen and Marky to try and make my way through this muddled life. To try and make the right decisions, to try not to hurt those I love and respect...to be the man I should be, not the man I seem to be. None of us can go back and start over, but we can all start today and make a new ending. This is what I want to do, use Clarence's example and hopefully make a new ending that I can be proud of.

While I'm on the subject of politicians, I'd like to discuss some other politicians you may not have heard of because they weren't from America and they're long gone now. Unfortunately, none of these men had any of the qualities Zebulon Baird Vance had, but they had a direct bearing on me and my family. The first of these so-called politicians was the evil Oliver Cromwell from England, who used Ireland as his own killing field to advance his political career in Britain. He murdered tens of thousands of Irish people (men, women and children), and uprooted more than that from their homes and deported them as slaves, for no other reason than because they were "Irish".

When the great potato blight and famine hit Ireland during the middle of the 1800's, Britain's overseer of Ireland at this time was a man named William Trevelyan. He decided that economic policy and "not coddling the poor" was more important than millions of people starving to death. But he was a saint compared to the worst landlord in Ireland during the Great Hunger period, Lord Duncan. There were over 500 child-skeletons found in workhouse mass graves on his property. And, he turned 10,000 people out of their homes in one city alone in County Mayo. Thousands starved to death as he ruthlessly cleared the land of "poor people".

I bring this subject up because the Great Potato Famine of the late 1840's in Ireland is the reason my great-great grandparents left the Emerald Isle and migrated to the United States. Specifically, to North Carolina and the garden spot of our beautiful state-- Robeson County. The deeds these awful men did cannot be excused, and cannot be overlooked in history. I'm so glad I'm an American, blessed to be able to live here; but I cannot help but grieve for the tens of thousands of people who didn't get the chance to live here, probably some long lost relatives who starved to death or were shipped off to lives of slavery because of these evil men.

On a recent trip to Ireland, I had the good fortune to discuss Irish politics and history with a very intelligent Irishman whom I respect. Our topics of conversation covered everything from the troubles in Northern Ireland, to whether Rory McElroy was Irish or British (he said when he won, he was Irish and when he lost, he was British); and finally to how this man personally felt about the English and how the English treated the Irish people throughout history. I expected venom and disgust from him regarding his thoughts on the English...I was wrong. He forgave them and said since they were neighbors, they needed to support each other and get along. He even admired Queen Elizabeth for her recent trip to Ireland

and for her support…he was a good man. My only issue with him was that he abandoned the national drink of Ireland, Guinness, and instead he was drinking a Bud Light in downtown Killarney, County Kerry! According to him, he loved imports!

"Brothers"

5

"Politicians are the same all over. They promise to build a bridge even when there is no river."

Politicians are indeed a strange crowd... seemingly, they'll tell you anything you want to hear, if it'll enhance their cause – maybe that's why so many of them are lawyers. Harry Truman was not a lawyer. I'm not sure he was even a politician, even though he ran for several offices and won races as a Senator, Vice-President and finally as the 33rd President of the United States. I've been to the Truman Presidential Library in Independence, Missouri; it's a fine place, full of history and items from the President's life. President Truman seems to have gained popularity over the years because people regarded him not so much as a politician, but as someone who told the truth, did the right thing and wasn't afraid to say so. He could never be a political candidate in today's world, he could never "spin" things to be popular; no, all he could do was to tell the truth and let the chips fall where they may.

As President, he once said, "All the president is, is a glorified public relations man who spends his time flattering, kissing, and kicking people to get them to do what they are supposed to do anyway." That statement wouldn't work well on Fox News these days. After he left office, he was asked his opinion of Richard Nixon. This was his reply: "Richard Nixon is a no good, lying bastard. He can lie out of both sides of his mouth at the same time, and if he ever caught himself telling the truth, he'd lie just to keep his hand in." This statement was well before Watergate, Truman could somehow see the dark side of Mr. Nixon.

When President Truman thought that the most popular war hero of his day, General Douglas McArthur, had disobeyed him during the Korean War, he fired him! He did not care about the political ramifications or the popular press...he did what he thought was right. That was the thing about Mr. Truman, you could trust him. You might not agree with him or even like him, but you knew when he told you something, he was telling you the truth – as he saw it. He said, "I remember when I first came to Washington. For the first six months you wonder how the hell you ever got here. For the next six months you wonder how the hell the rest of them ever got here." Tell it like it is Harry.

When he made the decision to drop the atomic bomb on Hiroshima to end WWII, he was criticized for doing it, and criticized for not doing more of it. He never let public opinion sway what he thought was the right thing to do, he never made decisions based on popularity – he did what he thought was right. He said, "You want a friend in Washington? Get a dog." He wasn't looking for friends, he was looking for the right thing to do for America. He often said, "When even one American—who has done nothing wrong—

is forced by fear to shut his mind and close his mouth – then all Americans are in peril."

My favorite quote from President Truman is this one, "I never gave anybody hell! I just told the truth and they thought it was hell." Amen brother.

———————

There are several other politicians I want to discuss before I move on to other subject areas, but before I get there, I want to briefly touch on the life of the best politician I've ever known personally…William B. Coleman. Bill was the Town Manager of Cary, N.C. for quite a while. I say was, because my friend died a few months ago from pancreatic cancer. A cruel disease which cheats life and does not play fair. I can describe this cancer as such, because it's true; but Bill never did. He never complained about this disease, never asked anyone I know why he got sick, never said anything about it being unfair, never cussed it out, screamed at it, or moaned about the unfairness of it all. At his funeral, there were testimonies of many people I didn't know and several from people I did know, and they all said the same thing – Bill fought as hard as he could, he was always positive, never feeling sorry for himself, trying at all times to ensure his friends and family were at ease and happy in whatever situations they were in. He seemed way more concerned over your troubles than his own. In fact, if you had not seen what the cancer was doing to his body, you would have never known his battle – he didn't talk about it.

Every person told a different story about Bill – preachers, teachers, politicians, friends, his son and even a total stranger who hadn't seen Bill in over 50 years, but who felt compelled to come to the service and tell how Bill had briefly touched his life so many years ago. We last visited Bill about two weeks before he died. He was nothing but a bag of bones – it broke our hearts to see our friend wasting away like this. At this time, he could only stay up and awake about 15 minutes at a time before laying back down and sleeping. But when we came, he stayed up over two hours with us and listened to stories and told stories and was vibrant and funny and never once complained about anything. He was a man of great faith and had seemingly accepted what the Lord had placed before him. Maybe Bill's final weeks and months were a lesson and a model for the rest of us to follow. How to endure with dignity, how to face life's struggles, how to accept reality and face the unthinkable – and do it all with grace and courage and compassion.

I've thought a lot about the last thing Bill said to me as we left his house that final day. He hugged us all, and it was sad feeling his once strong and vibrant body now reduced to a collection of brittle bones held together by a layer of skin. After he hugged me and looked directly in my eyes, he said, "See you soon."

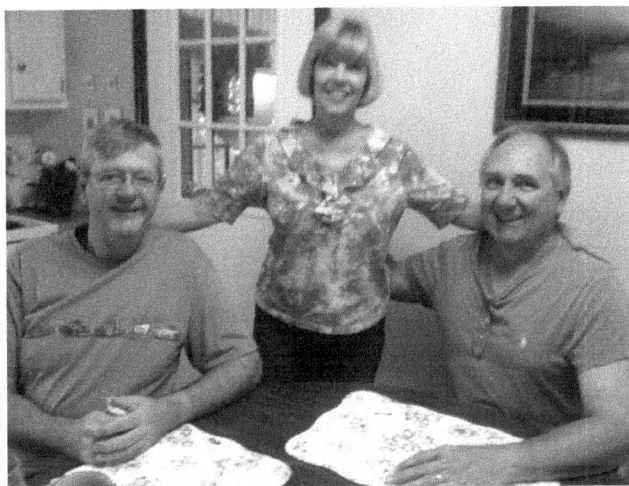

"homies"

6

"I've learned that people will forget what you said, people will forget what you did, but people will never forget how you made them feel."

This quote describes John Lennon for me. I can't remember things he said, nor what he did mostly, I can remember some of the lyrics he wrote...but I'll never forget how he made me feel. We are so impressionable when we're young, we're looking for something...anything to help us get through and understand life. John helped me. Oh, I know he was this, or that; and I know what he said about this or that...but that was just John. I'm not saying he was anything at all – I'm just saying I'll never forget how he made me feel.

He was not a good husband to Cynthia – far from it; he was not a good father to Julian – far from it. He would sometimes want to fight with his friends, he could be bombastic and crude and utterly vulgar. But there was something about John, something that if he touched you, then you remained touched and just ignored all the other stuff. He could write some of the most beautiful songs the world has ever known, with lyrics that could break your heart...then he could say or do some of the most cruel things imaginable.

I have a friend who is 65 years old, he has a hard time remembering the stories of our youth, even the stories from a few months ago. He's old and sedentary and conservative and for some unknown reason, has taken to listening to country music. However, several months ago I asked him what his favorite all time song was from the last 50 years or so...without hesitation, he said "Girl". John Lennon wrote that song and it has touched my friend's heart and soul now for 50 years. That's the best description of John that I can come up with...we can never forget how he made us feel. For those of you who have forgotten this little song...here it is: for you Larry.

Is there anybody going to listen to my story

All about the girl who came to stay?

She's the kind of girl you want so much

It makes you sorry

Still, you don't regret a single day

Ah, girl...girl

When I think of all the times I've tried so hard to leave her

She will turn to me and start to cry

And she promises the earth to me

And I believe her

After all this time I don't know why

Ah, girl...girl

She's the kind of girl who puts you down

When friends are there, you feel like a fool

When you say she's looking good

She acts as if it's understood

She's cool, cool, cool, cool

Girl...girl

Was she told when she was young that pain

Would lead to pleasure?

Did she understand it when they said

That a man must break his back to earn

His day of leisure?

Will she still believe it when he's dead?

Ah girl...girl Girl...girl.

"how bout them royals"

7

"If everything seems like it's under control, you're not going fast enough." - Mario Andretti

I have a friend named Don who's a foreigner...well, he's pretty much Americanized, but, he's still a foreigner. However, he's one of the most sensible men I know – he knows what's important in life and his goal is to pursue that to the ends of the earth. What's important is love. Don understands love and the importance it plays in our lives, he pursued it with a passion and once he found the true love of his life, he let no consequence hinder him from his goal of living forever with the woman of his dreams. I admire his passion and honesty and wish everyone could experience what Don has...true love. It can change your life.

Not only in a physical relationship, but in your quest for understanding the Lord as well. We are all searching for "something", we just don't quite understand exactly what it is that's missing in us. We were made with a hole in our hearts, a hole only God can fill, a yearning to know Him, to love Him and be with Him. A lot of people try to fill this void with all sorts of things that are totally useless and even harmful. They look for "things" to fill this void: drink, drugs, relationships, money, power, etc., etc. It never works. Only the love of the Lord fills this void, only

His love can make you happy, only His love can make you what you were meant to be. First, you must understand this…that this void can only be filled by the Lord; then, you'll understand how love can fill other parts of your life as well. If you're a man, how the love of a good woman can change your life—and vice versa. How the only thing that's important in your life is love.

Don made an important observation to me once. He said, "We all have two great questions to answer in our lives. What is worth living for? And, what is worth dying for? The answer to both, of course, is love."

Billy Graham is a man who understood love and the importance of it. First, love of the Lord, then of his wife Ruth. Mr. Graham started his "crusades" at a time of segregation in the United States, but in 1953 his insisted on integration for his revivals and crusades because the Lord loves all people. In 1957 he invited Martin Luther King, Jr. to preach jointly at a revival in New York City. It was Mr. Graham who bailed King out of jail in the 1960's when he was arrested in demonstrations. He has repeatedly been on Gallup's list of "most admired men and women". He has appeared on the list 55 times since 1955 (including 49 consecutive years), more than any other individual in the world.

One time, NBC offered him a $5 million contract to appear on television, but he turned it down in favor of continuing his touring revivals and crusades.

He had this longing in his heart to reach out to people to help fill the void in their hearts that he knew could only be filled by the Lord Jesus Christ. One person Mr. Graham reached was Louis Zamperini. Louis had gone to one of Mr. Graham's crusades in Los Angeles in 1949 at the urging of his wife. She wanted Louis to go to see if it could possibly change his life, which seemed to be on the verge of a total meltdown. Louis was consumed with rage, shame, violent flashbacks and constant nightmares. His drinking was out of control and his marriage was falling apart – all because of his incredible experience during WWII.

Louis grew up poor in Torrance, California, but became a track star and eventually competed in the 1936 Berlin Olympics in the 5,000 meter race. He then enlisted in the military in 1941 and became a bombardier. In 1943 his B-24 malfunctioned and crashed into the Pacific Ocean. Strafed by Japanese pilots and attacked by sharks, Zamperini and his pilot survived for 47 days in a rubber raft. Then things got worse. They were picked up by a Japanese ship and moved to a POW camp where Louis was starved, humiliated and savagely beaten almost to death.

After the war ended in 1945, he returned home but found no peace...that's when his wife urged him to go to Billy Graham's crusade. After hearing Mr. Graham preach about forgiveness and compassion and the love of Christ, Louis stopped drinking, repaired his marriage, forgave his Japanese captors and devoted himself to his faith and to helping troubled youngsters at a camp he founded. Active to the end of his life, Louis died of pneumonia at the age of 97. An incredible story, but how many other stories are similar to this, all because Billy Graham touched someone's life at one of his crusades?

Every President from Truman to Obama has called on him for advice (spiritual and otherwise), and his message remains the same...love the Lord your God with all your heart, soul and mind. Two diverse and totally opposite characters, Don Juan de Marco and Billy Graham, but both understanding the importance of love and its impact on our lives.

———————

There's another type of love I want to evaluate, but it's not love at all, really...we simply use the word "love" to express how deeply we feel about things. Such as, I "love" Krispy Kreme glazed doughnuts, or I love the beach, or the mountains, or the Wake Forest Demon Deacons. Well, I "love" some things like this as well. I love Tim Duncan. He's easy to love – he doesn't get in trouble with the police, doesn't abuse people, isn't in the headlines for misconduct or any other nonsense – he just seems to be a good guy. We were all introduced to Tim as a freshman basketball player at Wake Forest. When I saw his first game that year, I didn't know who he was; he was not a big name recruit at the time. Wake's head coach, Dave Odom, heard about him, and went to see him play a game. He could see the raw talent Tim possessed, and signed him to a scholarship – probably the best coaching move Dave ever made.

That first game Tim played was telling. We certainly didn't know him and were wary of Wake's history with big men...usually, they couldn't run very well, didn't have good hands, were weak and had very few skills. We soon realized Tim was not like these other big men. First of all, he could run up and down the court as fast as the guards, then he could actually catch the ball when they passed it to him. But the most special thing (for me) was that when any opponent tried a shot anywhere near Tim, he blocked it or altered the shot. His timing was impeccable. This was very unusual for any player, much less someone as tall as Tim. He didn't score much that first game, but those of us who witnessed the action, knew we had something special. And he didn't disappoint us.

In a time of "one and dones" (players who come to college for only one year, then turn pro), Tim stayed all four years at Wake. He could have easily turned pro after his sophomore year, certainly made millions of dollars after his junior year, but no, old Tim stayed. Only he can adequately answer why he chose to stay and wait to collect his millions of dollars; we're just glad he did. Player of the Year, ACC Championships, NCAA games it was truly a magical time in Wake Forest basketball history.

I went to a local sub shop one evening and Tim was in line with a couple of his buddies (back in his days at Wake). They were laughing and joking around – he was just one of the guys. I asked him if he'd autograph the bill of a cap I had, and he graciously did that: I later gave that cap to my niece Casey, I hope she still has it.

After graduation he carried the same qualities he had at Wake into the pros...loyalty, humility, passion and intensity. Most valuable player awards, NBA championships, All-star teams...he's done it all and all with one team. Tim is one of the few people – very few people – in the NBA today that can actually BE a role model. I love Tim Duncan and I'm grateful I have been able to witness his career and life...the life of a good man.

———

Long before Tim, I fell in love with another ACC basketball player – probably the best of them all – the incomparable David Thompson of N.C. State. Watching David play was akin to witnessing DaVinci paint, or Yo-Yo Ma play the cello – no one could do the things he could do on a basketball court – NO ONE! At only 6'4", it was said that If you left a dollar bill on top of the backboard, he could leap up, take the dollar bill in one hand and leave you four quarters with the other hand. I believe it.

He led State to an undefeated season one year and to the National Championship the next year...but even more substantial than that was that he beat UNC soundly those years as well – oh, how sweet that was. Yes, I loved David Thompson – he was the best of the best, someone God had laid a hand on and blessed with talent you simply don't see very often. None of us who were alive then will ever forget the game where NC State beat Maryland in triple overtime 103-100. Or the NCAA championship game when State beat UCLA, with the great Bill Walton...neither of those games could have been won by any team that did not have David Thompson on it – he was that good.

David went on to have an outstanding career in the NBA, but the temptations of fame and money led him to make some bad decisions that hurt his career. But, he's come back to be a leader in the NC State community and shown himself to be what he always was...special.

"I Will"

8

"Make everything as simple as possible, but not simpler."

Along with Krispy Kremes, Tim Duncan, David Thompson, Ireland, and Utah, I also love the Apostle Peter. Why him? Because he's so much like us. We have some of the qualities Peter had and it's easy for us to relate to some of the stories of him. Peter and his brother Andrew were fishermen – hard-working, probably a bit uneducated, simple laborers of that day and time. One day, they were on shore cleaning the nets after a day out at sea and Jesus walks by them, looks at them and says "follow me". They did. They stopped what they were doing, laid down their nets and followed Him. Now, honestly, I doubt I'd have done that. Somehow, some way, they must have known this man was special – the Bible is not clear how they knew that, but they followed the command of the Lord. Peter, like all the apostles, was a very ordinary man who was chosen to do extraordinary things.

He had periods of great faith and other periods of doubt, temper and selfishness – just like us! One day, Jesus told Peter and the others to get into the boat and cross over to the other side of the lake. They did just that and as Peter and his friends were on the boat crossing the sea, a storm arose and threatened to break apart the boat and drown all on board. Understandably, they were terrified – just like you and I would have been. But, in retrospect, think about it; if the Lord told you to get into the boat and go to the other side of the sea, then, no storm or anything else could have prevented you from doing that. If the Lord told you to go there, then you were going – storm or no storm! But, I totally understand being scared, just like Peter was. During the storm, they felt the end was near, and they noticed Jesus walking on the waves, coming towards them . Jesus told Peter to get out of the boat and walk on the water to Him. Peter did just that, but when he realized he was indeed walking on the water like Jesus was, his faith abandoned him and he began to sink. Jesus saved him, of course, then He stopped the wind and waves and calmed the storm as well.

We often trust the Lord to stop the storms in our lives, just as He did that night; and just like Peter, we too begin to doubt and start to sink because of unbelief. It's hard to remain steadfast in the face of a storm – whether that storm be temptation, ill health, death, divorce, trauma, or any number of things we face daily in our lives. Peter's example to us is to keep the faith, keep believing, no matter how bad the storm seems to be. If the Lord tells you to "go to the other side of the lake", then brother, you're going to the other side of the lake. Trust Him!

In Gethsemane, when the guards come to take Jesus away after Judas's betrayal, Peter loses his temper, takes his sword out and cuts off the ear of one of the guards. Jesus, of course, heals the man's ear and tells Peter to put his sword away...the only reason He has come to earth is die for us. But old Peter, just like us, loses his temper and does something crazy. The guards take Jesus away and Peter follows at a distance. Even though he's a little afraid now, Peter tells Jesus he will always be there and follow Him. Jesus looks directly at him and says "Peter, before the rooster crows, you will deny me three times." Of course, Peter vehemently denies this will ever happen and continues to follow Jesus at a safe distance. As Jesus is being questioned by the authorities, Peter is standing outside trying to see what's going to happen and someone accuses him of being one of Jesus's friends – Peter denies knowing Jesus. As the crowd closes in around him, he's asked two more times if he knows Jesus and Peter denies knowing Him all three times. As Peter answers for the third time, he hears the rooster crow and remembers Jesus's words to him.

Like Peter, we can all put on a brave front when we have to, and just like Peter, we can all lose our bravery and faith in times of peril and danger. When Jesus arose from the grave after three days, He told the women who saw Him first to go tell the apostles, specifically Peter, that He was here – He wanted to make sure Peter knew the good news. When Peter came and saw the risen Lord, Jesus asked Peter if he loved Him. Peter said, yes, of course he did. Then Jesus asked him twice more if he truly loved Him – three questions, for the three denials Peter gave earlier.

Yes, we're all like Peter – we struggle, we have periods of doubt, we're unsure of the future and what to do. Hopefully, we can all fight the good fight and continue to keep our faith, just as Peter did for the rest of his life, setting an example we're still following nearly 2000 years later.

——— ——— ———

Virgil Flowers is another man I admire, but for different reasons than Peter. I think old Virgil is a Christian, or, at least I think he wants to be a Christian – seemingly he struggles somewhat with this issue. I'm not really sure, since he seldom discusses his faith in public and I only occasionally see glimpses of it. Virgil is a detective, which means he deals with some unpleasant situations and nasty people at times – even dangerous people. He's also been divorced three times. In my opinion, the divorces are a result of his occupation and the demands it puts on his life and time away from home...but that's just my opinion.

In Virgil's job, he's allowed to dress casually, not in uniform, and he can usually be found in jeans, boots and vintage rock & roll tee shirts. He also lets his hair grow a tad longer than his superiors would like, but he gets the job done and catches bad guys and they like that more than his appearance. And speaking of his appearance, old Virgil seems to have the look that the ladies like. He certainly has no problems catching the attention of the female population...it may be the jeans and Steely Dan tee shirts, or the longish hair, I'm not sure – but whatever it is, it's working. He tells me he's unsure whether there will be a fourth Mrs. Flowers or not; the last Mrs. Flowers left a rather unpleasant memory for him.

I do know for sure that he does not mind testing the waters and making himself available, but seemingly, long term romances are not in his plans right now. I also know from being in his car and in his house, that he reads his Bible frequently. I've made mental notes of where the bookmark was, and it's usually in different spots from one day to the next. I'm sure Virgil is a believer, but I'm also sure he has questions and I'm not so sure he's found the answers yet – but he's looking, which is a good thing.

I like Virgil, we're friends and confidants; he's a bit younger than me, but we have similar views of the world and politics and music – and we both used to be athletes. For some strange reason, he's chosen to take up fishing now, instead of golf or tennis, but, it seems to relax him and gives him time alone on a lake to think. I'm pretty sure there are times when he doesn't actually try to catch anything, he just wants the time alone with his thoughts and questions and the never ending search for answers to those questions. I hope he finds them.

"My Twin"

9

"Where are we going? And why am I in this handbasket?"

Years ago, many years ago, my hometown held a minor league tennis tournament of sorts outside of town on some clay courts. They did a good job of organizing it and promoting it, but ultimately not a lot of people wanted to come out there and watch a bunch of young guys from New Zealand or Argentina or Romania or Timbuctu that they've never heard of, or would never hear of again. I did.

One of the reasons I enjoyed it was because of the tennis, but also because they usually brought in past tennis stars to play exhibition matches. That's what I really enjoyed. Seeing the great Stan Smith, the flamboyant John Newcombe, players you'd always read about as a kid – it was great. My good friend Amy Franklin was a volunteer at the tournament and helped arrange court times and transportation and things like that for the players. She was just out of college, and being very young, she really didn't know who most of the old guys were who were playing the exhibition matches.

Amy invited me to come out early one day and hang around with her before the matches started and watch the guys warm up. I found her and she got us a couple of free Diet Pepsi's and we sat in the stands drinking and talking as the players were all milling around. Finally, Stan Smith (who was 6'4") came out on court with a short little spindly, old guy. EVERY player out there stopped what they were doing and stood around the court and watched. They started hitting rhythmically back and forth, back and forth – center of the strings, no miss hits, beautiful to watch. The players standing around the courts were mesmerized – as was I. Amy finally said, "I'm surprised all these young guys have stopped what they're doing to watch Stan Smith and that little bow-legged guy hit balls...I mean, I barely even remember Stan Smith."

Amy, Amy Amy...poor little girl. These guys aren't here to watch Stan Smith, as great as he might be; they've all stopped what they're doing to watch the little 5'8" bow-legged guy, best player in the history of tennis, hit balls...the incomparable Rod Laver. At this point in his life, Laver's legs were arthritic and he couldn't move well, so being the gentleman that he was, Stan Smith hit every ball right back to him so Laver didn't have to do anything except unleash those beautiful groundstrokes of his that were legendary. Amy had heard the name Rod Laver, but she really didn't know who he was.

Who he was, was the best tennis player of all-time. The only player to win the Grand Slam twice, in 1962 and again in 1969. He would have won it more if he'd been allowed to play. After winning it the first time in 1962, he turned pro and was prevented from playing any of the Grand Slams tournaments, which were held only for amateurs at the time. When they started letting the pros play in them in 1969, he won it again. For 6 years, in the prime of his career, he was prevented from playing in the sport's greatest events: Wimbledon, the U.S. Open, the French Open and the Australian Open.

In 1962, he won a record 22 singles titles in a single season, but that was in the "amateur" days, when players only got travelling money paid under the table. It was hard to support yourself that way, so Laver (and a lot of the others) all turned pro in 1963 and started the pro tour as we know it today. In 1967 he married Mary Benson, who was a divorcee with three children. Taking on that responsibility had to be financially burdensome for Laver, but you can't control who you love – and he loved Mary. They later had a son of their own and stayed happily married for 46 years until Mary died at the age of 84.

When tennis decided to let the pros play again in 1969, Laver won all four Grand Slams for the second time. He also won 18 of the 32 tournaments he entered that year, with a win-loss record of 106-16. He also won innumerable doubles tournaments and mixed-doubles tournaments – he was The Man. He was also the first player to ever break the $100,000 barrier in a year. He ultimately won over 200 tournaments, and won a record 45 open titles after he turned 30 years old…no wonder his knees were a little arthritic.

You take all the criteria – longevity, playing on grass and clay and hardcourts, amateur, professional, his behavior, his appearance… everything. He is the best player of all time, and I'm sitting here in awe watching him hit tennis balls 20 yards away from me. After 15-20 minutes of non-stop volleying, he and Stan walked off the court and were surrounded by the young players. Amy suddenly got up and went down there as well with her plastic Diet Pepsi cup. She stood in line and coaxed the greatest tennis player of all time to sign her cup…and he did. Then, my great friend Amy came back up in the stands and gave me the cup. What a friend, what a girl; I still have my Rod Laver cup, I'll treasure it for a long, long time. For the memory of that great man, and for the memory of my great friend.

"To Bill"

10

"There are two kinds of people in the world. Those who wake up in the morning and say, "Good morning Lord." And, there are those who wake up in the morning and say, "Good Lord, it's morning."

Being rather old, like I am, has given me the opportunity to know and experience several preachers (or pastors) over the years. As a group, they've all been good men and women – as far as I know. I'm pretty sure being a preacher is a tough job...people falling asleep during your sermons, impossible to keep all the congregation happy, always visiting people, listening to complaints, trying to keep the peace, performing funerals and maybe even worse – performing weddings. Question: if a preacher has counseled two young people about marriage, but in his heart (through his experience), feels that it's a bad idea for them to marry, should he refuse to marry them? Or, go ahead with the service? I hope they teach preachers about these types of issues in seminary, or preacher college – certainly, they face a lot of tough situations in their duties.

I've never personally consulted a preacher with any problems – not that I haven't had any, just that I was usually too stupid to seek advice from anyone smarter than me. The first preacher I remember was from the First Baptist Church in my hometown of Red

Springs...a truly wonderful man who's face and voice I can still remember nearly 50 years later, James O. Mattox. Mr. Mattox baptized me and most of my friends (by dunking us...the Baptist way). He would arrange beach trips for our youth groups and come along to chaperone as well – good luck with that. Most of the boys were okay on those trips, but there were a few who were labeled as "shenanigators" – they know who they are. But, Mr. Mattox loved us all.

He had a brother who was in the movies, Gregory Walcott. I'm not sure why he changed his name from Mattox to Walcott, but I guess that's fairly common in Hollywood. What's uncommon, was that Mr. Walcott was also a preacher. Mr. Mattox would have his brother come to our little church and preach "revivals" during the summer. I'll bet you didn't have a movie star preach in your church, did you? We were special. Mr. Walcott seemed to be a friend of Clint Eastwood's out in Hollywood; seemingly he appeared in most of Clint's movies. He was never a star, but he was always active and had a full resume of pictures and films.

Mr. Mattox had a great influence on a lot of people, including my little group of friends...we still talk about him today when we gather, and we're still grateful for the effort he made to get my friend Larry enrolled at Wake Forest. A good old Baptist boy going to a good old Baptist school...what could go wrong there? Nothing my friends...absolutely nothing.

Well, after a lot of us sort of grew up, I guess Mr. Mattox grew lonely and started looking for a new challenge and he moved to Rutherfordton, to pastor a church in the remote hinterlands of western North Carolina. We missed him and were greatly influenced by him; I hope he somehow knew the impact he had on a bunch of young, punk kids in rural Robeson County, re-living his memory 45-50 years down the road.

David Morrow followed Mr. Mattox in Red Springs…big shoes to fill. He was there during my early college years when I was a tad rebellious and a lot weird looking. But Mr. Morrow didn't mind, he liked me…I don't know why, I guess it's the job of preachers to like everyone, even me. I had a project in a Sociology class I was taking that required me to somehow procure a meeting place for people and discuss current issues. I didn't know how to do that, but I asked Mr. Morrow and he volunteered a room at the church for me and my weird looking friends to use once a week. Thinking back now, it would not surprise me if the church members were not real happy with his decision…but, it all worked out.

Years later, after I moved to Winston-Salem and was looking for a church to attend, I decided I'd try a Baptist church I'd seen fairly close to my condo, Old Town Baptist Church. I didn't know anything about this church, other than it was Baptist – like me. My first day there, I walked in and sat down in the pew and looked up to see Mr. Morrow standing up front. Incredibly enough, he had left Red Springs to become the new preacher at Old Town Baptist. We had a grand old reunion, he was a fine man and I liked him and respected him a lot. Unfortunately, he wasn't there very long…something about internal politics and the mess associated with it. I was sad to see him leave.

I want to mention two other preachers, both of whom shall remain nameless, for the simple fact that I've forgotten their names. One was very good, the other one was not so good. First, the good one. He was a fill-in preacher at Knollwood Baptist Church, while they were searching for a permanent pastor. From what I remember, he was a professor at some seminary who taught preaching…and boy, was he a good one. He had me fully alert and hanging on every sentence he preached. When the sermon ended, I was always disappointed, I truly wanted him to keep on speaking. This man was indeed a gifted speaker and I hope his students will be able to capture the essence of his style.

The second preacher needed some lessons from the first guy. I only went once, so maybe he just had a bad day…we all do; but once was enough. The sermon started out routinely enough, then he started to get all choked up about something (insignificant, as I remember), then it went from gently crying to all out sobbing in the end. It was very uncomfortable and just a touch weird, in my opinion. I won't mention the church, because I don't want to unduly bring any criticism here…but it was very disconcerting for me and I never went back.

I loved our new preacher at Old Town Baptist, Wade Dellinger. I've mentioned Wade before – truly a gifted speaker and Bible scholar. He would be preaching, standing behind the pulpit, and he would quote scripture verses and anecdotes, and historical facts and all sorts of stuff...truly evident that he'd spent a lot of time preparing the message. My wife, Susan, was singing in the choir then; the choir loft was behind the preacher...I was telling her how impressed I was with Wade's message, all the work he must've done to find that information and relay it to us. She said, "Well, you know he doesn't use notes don't you?" What? He doesn't use notes? How can remember all that stuff? How can he recite those verses (often many consecutive verses at once)? How can he keep his message in order and remember everything? I don't know the answers to any of these questions, but he did. I guess he had a gift, or was blessed in some special way...but my respect for him grew proportionately as I watched him thereafter, knowing he was speaking from his memory and mind and spirit – and not any notes.

On through the years I'll progress, only mentioning one more preacher...my first experience with a female preacher. Anne Elmore was a good pastor. I was a little concerned about a woman preacher – us Baptists are very old fashioned at times. However, this was a Methodist church Anne was leading, even though she told me she grew up Baptist – trying to comfort me a little, I think. After a few weeks, I caught her alone after church one day and asked her a question I simply had to know the answer to, if I was to continue attending. "Did she believe every single word in the Bible was true?"

She looked at me very directly, then looked up towards the ceiling for about 5 seconds, then back at me and said, "Yes, I do." That was enough for me, she's a good old girl. Unfortunately, the Methodist church likes to move their preachers around after 4-5 years (why, I truly don't know), but they moved Anne and we were very sad to see her leave – I miss my woman preacher. From Mr. Mattox all the way to a female pastor – I've been able to experience it all...I guess I'm just lucky that way.

"Princess Kali"

11
"I have often regretted my speech, never my silence."

I'm lucky enough to have an extraordinary group of friends, but I could've had even more friends if I'd made the effort and not been so selfish. I feel like I have to explain one of these lost opportunities. It's bothered me over the years and maybe writing about it will ease some of my guilt over this incident. This was during the period between marriages when I was totally into tennis. I played virtually every day and was involved in USTA team tennis as well. There was a guy at my condominium complex that I got to know through tennis and we became pretty good friends. His name was Jeff.

Jeff and I started to hang around a lot at the pool, playing tennis with each other, just enjoying each other's company. He wasn't a great tennis player, but good enough that we could hit with each other and laugh and talk – like friends do. Jeff had been dating the same young lady for several months and they were planning on getting married soon. He asked me if I'd be an usher at his wedding. Sure I would, I was honored that he asked. They hadn't set a date yet, but I was sure it would all work out.

In the meantime, our tennis team was doing very well. We won the city championship again and were scheduled to go to the state finals again, this time being held in Charlotte in the following month. Then I got the news from Jeff that his wedding was planned on a Saturday, the following month, which would be the same day that the finals of the state tournament would be held. Hmmm. Well, I thought about this and even discussed it with Jeff. First of all, our team would have to make it through the early rounds during the week to have a chance at playing on Saturday in the finals. Then, even if we did make the finals, they were always played at 9:00 on Saturday mornings; his wedding wasn't until 3:00 Saturday afternoon. If I made it to the finals, I could still easily get back in time for the wedding.

Well, our team made it to the finals, with me playing No. 1 singles and, yes, we were scheduled to play at 9:00 Saturday morning in the finals, with an opportunity to go to the regional finals in Tennessee. I brought my suit with me, so I could shower and change and go directly to the wedding after the tennis. Then, disaster struck. It started to sprinkle rain...not very hard, just enough that prevented us from starting the tennis on time. We were told to "wait it out". I began to get very nervous as rain continued; then I just wanted it to rain hard and cancel everything so I could leave – that didn't happen.

About 10:30 or so, the rain stopped and it cleared up and they started drying the courts. I had a discussion with my teammates about my wedding plans that day. They told me that my first commitment had been to the team – we'd played all season long for this opportunity – I could not abandon them on the last day! All eight of them were pleading with me to stay and fulfill my duty to them and help realize our goals. I should not have listened to them...but I did.

I didn't even get on the court till nearly noon, then had a long three set match which didn't finish till nearly 2:00. It was still an hour and a half drive back to Winston Salem. I had missed the wedding, let down my friend and totally humiliated myself – for tennis! This was pre-cell phone days, and I didn't know how to call him at the church – he wasn't at his condo, obviously. I had made a terrible decision and I felt completely humiliated and remorseful.

Jeff's marriage, I found out later, went off beautifully, no problems, I wasn't missed in the least – except that he and I both knew I'd let him down and chosen my own selfish reasons over the most important day in his life. After he returned from his honeymoon, I tried to see him and talk to him, but it wasn't the same. He wasn't rude to me (he was too much the gentleman for that), but he just didn't want to talk to me, or play tennis with me, or anything with me. There's no excuse for what I did, and I still regret this 26 years later. I tried to call Jeff a few times, hoping the months, even years would smooth things out – it was never the same. I had lost the opportunity to be friends with a good man.

I have never forgotten this, and I'm sure I never will; each time my selfishness arises now, I remember what it cost me all those years ago. So, when my friend Larry wants me to go to a soccer match with him – I'll go. When Jerry wants me to visit and go to a UNC-P football game with him – I'll go. When Dickie wants to go to some minor league baseball games – I'm in. When Marky wants to hang out in an Irish bar and watch hurling matches – I'll be there. And, when Allen wants to go over to Pembroke and look for some trouble – well...let me think about that one.

─── ─ ─ ─ ───

I have another friend who's important to me. Although I haven't actually met David yet, I know one day I will...and I'm really looking forward to it. Kind David lived about 3000 years ago, but his influence on me and millions of others is untold. He was a truly gifted man...an acclaimed warrior, musician, poet and author of the Book of Psalms in the Bible. He was described by God Himself as "a man after my own heart". As the youngest of his father's sons, David spent his youth tending sheep, but his greatness could not be kept in the pastures. When the giant Goliath was shouting insults at King Saul and the Israelites and frightening all those on the battlefield, it was David who picked up a smooth stone, placed it in his slingshot and killed the giant, against all odds.

It was only David's musicianship that could comfort King Saul in times of trouble, it was David who led Israel's armies to victories and made him so famous in the land that the King sought to have him killed because he was jealous of the shepherd boy. He eventually outlasted Saul and became the King of Israel and brought the Ark of the Covenant to Jerusalem, intending to build a temple. But David got complacent, David got lazy and David became lustful...just like most other human beings before and after him...just like us today.

David was a warrior king, his job was to lead his armies in battle, to set the example and to be the man God meant him to be. But, during the battle of Rabbah, instead of leading his armies, David stayed home. One day, he went up to his roof to get some air and saw a beautiful, young woman bathing on her roof next door to him. He sent his guards over to her requesting her presence before him. Her name was Bathsheba and she soon became pregnant with David's child. The problem was that Bathsheba and David were both married to other people at the time, Bathsheba's husband being one of the David's leading commanders at the ongoing battles. David sent for Bathsheba's husband, Uriah, to bring him back and coerce him to "lay" with Bathsheba in hopes he could convince everyone the unborn child was Uriah's and not his. David's deception did not work, so instead, he sought to have Uriah killed by sending him back to the front lines and ordering him to attack a superior foe and position. Uriah's ultimate death did nothing but to further displease the Lord.

Here was David, "a man after God's own heart" who has now committed adultery and murder. If a man as gifted and committed as David can fall so far, how do we normal people ever have a chance? Without the Lord, we don't. We will all fail, we will all commit sins – hopefully not adultery and murder – but we will sin, it's inevitable. All we can do is to keep trying to live the good life, keep praying when temptations arise, keep Christ's example forefront in our mission, and when we fail, ask for forgiveness and learn from our mistakes. God loves us, just as He loved David; He wants us to succeed, He wants us to join Him in heaven for an eternity and commune with Him. It's up to us the directions we take in life. We will all sin, but will we all learn from our mistakes, ask the Lord's forgiveness and live in eternity with Him, as David ultimately did?

"Susan and Me"

12

"Any fool can criticize, condemn and complain, and most fools do."

I've written about Mickey Mantle before – it's easy for me to do since he was a boyhood idol of mine for many years. Hopefully, I won't re-hash those other stories here, but I can't seem to get Mickey out of my mind. He was so great, so gifted and so talented that it made him seem super-human to us normal people. He wasn't. He had just as many faults as the rest of us, he was just a better athlete than we were. It's well documented the struggles he had with alcoholism, the he way treated his wife, his infidelities, the way he neglected his children...yes, I'm aware of all that. But in the end, before he died, he asked for forgiveness of those things, he knew he'd made mistakes and wanted people to know he was truly remorseful. In my opinion, it took a lot of guts to do that, and I respected him for it.

As I previously recorded, I saw him play once, and it was something I'll never forget. I also met him once – again, a moment that'll never be forgotten. After he retired, he lent his name to a chain of men's stores called appropriately "Mickey Mantle's Men's Store". One was opening at the Holly Hills Mall in Burlington when I was a student at Elon College, which was just a few miles away. Since I didn't have a car, I convinced my friend Ritchie Beam to drive us over there to meet the Mick.

We could see Mickey standing in front of the store, with a line of idol worshippers going way around the corner. We got in line and waited our turn, as we got close we could read the sign up front that said, "No autographs, don't ask Mr. Mantle to sign anything." Bummer. So I put my pen and paper up and just watched him...it was amazing simply to watch him. The line moved rather quickly, seemingly you walked up to him and shook his hand and he said, "How ya doing?" That was the extent of the conversation. I understood, there wasn't time for him to actually talk to the hundreds of people lined up there. So, here we go, closer and closer..."How ya doing? How ya doing? How ya doing?" Finally, it's my turn; I'm two feet from one of the best baseball players in history, two feet from my all-time sports hero; he has on a short sleeve shirt and his forearms look like they're bigger than my legs, his shoulders look like he has on shoulder pads and his face could be the model for Greek gods. His hand engulfs mine, he squeezes it and says "How ya doing?" Before I can answer or even breathe, I'm pushed along the end of the line. We didn't actually go in the store and buy anything; obviously a lot of people didn't, because the chain closed in a year or two. But by God I shook Mickey Mantle's hand and he spoke directly to little old me. "How ya doing?" Mick...I'm doing just great!

I was also fortunate enough to meet George Harrison one day when I was in London. Susan and I had just come up the stairs from the subway when we saw him entering a restaurant across the street from us. We scampered across the street and peered inside the window, and sure enough, there was George seated all by himself looking at a menu. I started to go inside and Susan grabbed my arm and said, "What are you doing?" I said, "I'm going in and talk to him…how often does anyone ever get to speak to a Beatle?" "Well, you'll just be embarrassed when they kick you out, "she said, "I'm not going in, I'll wait out here for them to boot you out." Okay, but I have to try.

I go in and walk up to his table and he never looks up from the menu. I sort of clear my throat, he still doesn't look up; I cough, he still doesn't look up; then I say "George!" He looks up. I had nothing beyond that planned. As I waited for the restaurant people to urge me out the door, George says, "Do you want to sit down?" "Really?" I say. "Only if you're hungry," he said. So I sat down.

Just as I took my seat, the waitress came over and George ordered a hamburger and chips and Coke…she looked at me and I said, "I'll have what he's having." I looked at him and said, "I thought you were a vegetarian." He said, "No, that's Paul, I like a good hamburger. I tried being veggie for a while, but, all things must pass…I just missed it too much." I totally understood.

He said it was okay to ask him a few questions while he ate...so I did. My mind was racing so fast, I couldn't remember stuff and just asked what popped in my mind at the time; I wish I'd had time to plan a proper interview, but, it is what it is, and here's a summary of our conversation:

Did Yoko really break you guys up? No...well, sort of...umm, no. We were all kind of tired of the Beatles thing and wanted to do our own stuff...but, she urged it along I must say.

What is John really like? Really? You're sitting here talking to ME and you want to know what John is like?

Oh...sorry; but, what's he like? Next question!

What's your favorite Beatles song? "I, Me, Mine" would be first, then my next favorite would be "Number 9"

Really? No, I'm just messing with you...I hated that piece of crap.

Would you like to get together with Paul and Ringo and record some more? No.

Okay...why not? Because Paul's an insolent hack, too full of himself and Ringo's old and worn out.

Wow...I had no idea. I'm just messing with you again mate. Can't you take a joke?

Oh, I thought you were supposed to be the serious Beatle? I am the serious Beatle, seriously messing with you.

Well George, there's really one thing I've always wanted to know...sorry mate, I've got to run, maybe next time.

There'll be a next time????? Of course, here's my number, give me a call anytime.

What, What, WHAT!!!! I've been what? Talking in my sleep? Oh...sorry guys, just ignore these last several paragraphs.

"sweet"

13
"I am not young enough to know everything."

I've always liked Queen Elizabeth II of England. She has seemed like a good person and if it weren't for her being a queen, I think she'd be just like one of us...sort of. She was born in 1926 and came to the throne in 1952 when her dad, King George VI, died. Being relatively unknown outside Britain at the time, her life changed forever at that moment. Twenty-six years old and Queen of the British Empire with over 32 countries under her realm...what were you doing at age 26?

Today, she looks like a queen should look, regal and dignified. But in the 1950's, she was, in the terminology of Paul McCartney, "Hot". She was indeed a very attractive woman – and a brave one as well. During WWII, she joined the Women's Auxiliary Territorial Service, where she trained as a driver and mechanic and was promoted after five months on duty. After the war she married Prince Philip of Greece and Denmark. She'd met him earlier in her life, in 1939, when she was only 13 years old. She said she fell in love with him when they started exchanging letters.

Philip had no financial standing and was foreign-born. Some of the King's advisors did not think him good enough for her. He was a prince without a home or kingdom. But, Elizabeth loved him and they married at Westminster Abbey in 1947 and have been together ever since. The Queen has a deep sense of religious and civic duty and takes her oath seriously. She worships at the Church of England and with the national Church of Scotland.

She is the patron of over 600 organizations and charities and personally handles about 430 engagements each year. For much of her life she has surrounded herself with dogs especially corgis; but she also loves horses – riding them and attending the races. It's also rumored that Elizabeth likes to spend her free time reading mysteries, working on crossword puzzles and even watching wrestling on television. I know she has a good sense of humor. When the Beatles gave a command performance for the Royals early in their career, before one song John urged everyone to clap along, and for those up front (the Royals) to "rattle their jewelry". I guess she could've beheaded him for that – but she liked John.

She is now the longest-lived and second-longest reigning monarch of the United Kingdom; she'll surpass Queen Victoria in September, 2015. However, she's had two threats to her life – that we know about. In June, 1981, she was riding her horse in the Trooping of the Colour, a special military parade to celebrate her birthday, when a man in the crowd pointed a gun at her. He fired, but the gun was loaded with blanks and the queen was not hurt. The following year an intruder broke into Buckingham Palace and confronted Elizabeth in her bedroom. The press had a field day with that, wondering where Philip was.

I admire the queen. Certainly she's had as many family problems (maybe more) as the rest of us have, and her husband can be quite inconsiderate at times. The queen once said, "Grief is the price we pay for love". She's had her share of grief – just like the rest of us, and I wish her well. She's a good queen and I think she really tries hard to connect with everyone, just like the time at a palace reception when she asked Eric Clapton, "Have you been playing a long time?" Yep, she's a good old queen.

"Like Father, Like Daughter"

14

"The problem with stealing quotes off the internet is you never know if they are genuine." - Abraham Lincoln

We were riding around Ireland one beautiful, rainy, cold day – lost, as usual – when we noticed a little pub called the South Pole Inn, located in the little village of Annascaul, County Kerry. Since we were lost and thirsty we stopped at the South Pole Inn for beverages and directions...I'm sure glad we did. The pub was named by the man who first opened it many years ago, Tom Crean. Here's the story of why he named it The South Pole Inn:

Tom Crean enlisted in the Royal Navy before his 16th birthday. He was a strong, hard worker with a cheerful disposition, and liked by all who met him. In 1910, he joined the Terra Nova expedition under Commander Scott to explore Antarctica (then, virtually unexplored and unknown). With Scott, they came within 150 miles of the Pole (no one had been to South Pole yet), when Crean and two others were ordered to return to the base camp, 800 miles away. This journey, made in temperatures ranging from -25 degrees to -50 degrees was filled with danger. One of the three men developed scurvy and 100 miles from base camp was no longer able to stand unaided. Crean and the other man pulled him on a sled to within 35 miles of safety. Then, weakened by fatigue and hunger, Crean left the dying man in the care of his companion, while Crean attempted to cross the final 35 miles of the journey alone in an effort to reach help. Following an 18 hour non- stop march – made in -40 degree weather, Crean reached the base camp, secured help for his two friends, and rescued them from the certain death they were facing.

Crean would make a total of three Antarctic expeditions, the last being with the explorer Sir Ernest Shakleton in 1913. That journey ended in disaster – the crew was left on an ice floe, stranded for 7 months. Finally, Shakleton picked Crean, himself, and another man to make a daring attempt to get help. Weak, poorly equipped and inadequately clothed, they traveled for 36 straight hours without rest, finally arriving at a whaling station where they sought help for the others they left behind.

Tom Crean retired from the Navy in 1920 and returned to Annascaul where he married and settled. He and his wife bought and rebuilt the building that now houses the South Pole Inn. He spent the rest of his life enjoying family life and eschewed the many attempts by visitors to engage him in tales of his exploits in the Antarctic. His tale is only known because of the book written about it by one of the men Crean saved, "Hearts of Lions".

Tom Crean died in 1938 from a ruptured appendix. This seemingly indestructible man was finally laid to rest in the tiny cemetery in his home town, in a tomb he built himself, overlooking the hills of Kerry. Later, in our journey around the wilds of Kerry, we came upon the Dingle Brewery, located in the scenic little village of Dingle. This brewery had just opened in the last few months and featured only one brew at the time…Tom Crean Lager, a bold brew in honor of one of Kerry's and Ireland's greatest men.

"two great men"

15

"It's more fun to be a pirate than to join the navy."

I've got too much stuff in my house — not furniture, just stuff that's not important to anyone but me. I need to get rid of at least half of it. I made an attempt recently to do just that. I went through closets, desks, containers, the basement, bookshelves and other hidden places and came up with exactly half a trash bag. I can't seem to force myself to discard any of this junk I've got...well, it's not really junk, a lot of it is pretty valuable in fact — and sentimental. I've got loads and loads of Beatles stuff — records, lunchboxes, Beatles cards, magazines, pictures, about 100 Beatles books, Beatles collector plates, little figurines, Beatles tins and boxes, and about a dozen Beatles matryoshka dolls Susan brought me back from Russia. I also have some Beatles autographs — I will never get rid of those. Two from Paul, two from George, two from Ringo, and one from John. These will stay with me for the duration.

I don't really understand why autographs are important to people, but they are. I've often held John Lennon's autograph in my hands and stared at it and run my fingers over his name — does that seem weird? Heck, I've done the same thing with Edward Abbey's autographs, which I'll also keep for the duration. I have an autographed copy of a book by

Michael Crichton, in fact, he made it to me personally because my sister asked him to, and he did it – she's special that way. I have Paul Hornung's autograph in a book he wrote, and I had Tim Duncan's autograph, but as you now know – I gave it away.

My five great friends autographed an earlier book I wrote, and I treasure that memento as I do a letter I have from my mother that she wrote me about 35 years ago. She had a wonderful and distinct handwriting that I just love to look at – I'm a little biased I guess. I don't have any letters or writings from my father or grandfather or grandmother – I wish I did; I'd trade those last two for any of my Beatles autographs – I think I would – yeah, I'm pretty sure I would (at least for one of Ringo's).

I've got over 100 books on the American Indians and the Indian Wars. My goal is to donate them to Pembroke State University, or as it's now known, UNC-Pembroke. UNC...can you believe that? To me it'll always be Pembroke State – proud to be a Brave! The library has let me know they'd love to have my collection and I'd love to clean out that bookcase, I just need Jerry to come up here and box them all up and take them all down there – you know how I am. I've got about 400-500 other books that I've read over the years, all collecting dust in bookcases throughout the house. Why do you feel the need to keep books you've already read? I don't know.

I've got Indian statues all around the house, pottery, paintings, pictures, little wooden boxes, big plastic tubs full of old, worn out pictures, high school junk, college junk, trophies (what in the world good are they?), petrified wood, rocks from Ireland, dirt from Ireland, coins from Ireland and even a lucky token from Ireland – I'm still waiting for it to work.

Susan never complains, except when she has to dust all this crap. She's a good old girl. I've saved newspapers, magazines, pictures, pens, pencils, rubber bands, watches, glasses, sunglasses, cups, coffee cups, baseball cards, football cards, basketball cards, old golf balls, new golf balls, I even have a ceramic football! Why, Gary? Why can't you get rid of this junk? Please, will someone help me answer this question...why?

"yep"

16

"Egotist: A person more interested in himself than in me."

Retirement. You work your entire life to get there, then what? Golf? Fish? Putter around the yard? Play with the grandbabies? I've been a student of retirement for several years now, it's something I've thought of often – not exactly dreamed of, just thought about it. We've all heard the stories of people who work all their lives, save their money, invest well, retire – then die 6 months later. That's probably happened to a few people – I don't know any of those people personally. I think they would have probably died those 6 months later, whether they retired or not. At least they got 6 months of not having to go to work, not having that pressure, not having to put up with terrible bosses and selfish co-workers. Not having to fight the morning traffic, drinking bad coffee and going to boring, interminable, senseless meetings. I'd take 6 months of that...yes, indeed.

All people are different. My lovely little wife retired after 38 years in the school system. She stayed home for 6 months, got bored, then started back working part-time with the schools, which has almost morphed into full time – it might as well be, she certainly has the headaches of a full time job. But, she's different, and she was still young when she retired. I've come to realize retirement's different for everyone, and the criteria and reasons for retirement differ from person to person. My wife's dad retired at age 70 because he wanted to do other things while he was still in good health. He traveled, he joined stock clubs, he bought a new house, he had a full slate of activities to keep him active and busy. And, 23 years later, he's still going strong – he retired at the exact right time for him.

I also know a guy who drove a truck his entire career, nearly 40 years of fighting traffic, listening to irate customers, crazy supervisors and idiotic dispatchers. He couldn't wait to get away from the madhouse of that job. He fished for 4 months until he nearly went crazy from boredom, went back to the same job (they knew he'd be back), and is as happy as he can be. He needed it. He needed the daily contact with people and the routine and the "busyness" of it all. He was different, just like we all are.

My friend Jerry recently retired and is loving it. I'm so happy for him. He retired from a job that required him to work six days a week and all day on Saturday! That's just not right. He is so busy in his retirement now, I've kidded him that he's going to have to go back to work to have some free time. Retirement was, and is, perfect for him. He's found time to paint his front door, hang pictures, mess in the yard, cut down a tree, wash the cars, clean out the attic...wait a minute – this is retirement? Well, it's working for old Jer; doesn't seem that idyllic to me, but as you know, I'm different.

Another good and old friend, Larry, has also retired and doesn't miss work one iota. He's built a swimming pool in his back yard, babysits grandbabies, does odd jobs for his kids and wife, monitors all Wake Forest sports websites, and from Jacksonville, keeps me informed of any happenings and news in my hometown of Winston-Salem...he's valuable that way. Retirement has seemingly been a seamless transition for old Larry; it's given him time to think about things, to reflect on life's greater meanings and to formulate his ideas on what's important and what's not so important. I won't attempt to place any value judgments here, because I know what he decides is the exact right decision for him. He's smart that way.

Our friend Bill never did retire, I wish he would have; I wish he could have done some more things with us and with his son – but that's just my opinion. Bill did what was right for him. He worked until cancer robbed him of the rest of his life. He certainly could've retired sooner, he just chose not to...and who are we to argue with that? Each man (or woman) must make their own choices and only they know what is right for them. So many variables to consider – savings, pensions, social security, happiness, personal relationships, on and on – many unknown and even secret desires affect everyone's decisions. What I would have wanted for Bill didn't mean a hill of beans compared to what Bill wanted for Bill. I truly don't think our friend had any regrets about any of the decisions he made in his life –

retirement, or otherwise. Wouldn't it be nice to say the same thing about ourselves one day?

Some people are "forced" into retirement...I use the term loosely. It's more due to the circumstances in their lives that make choices for them. My friend Allen is the prime example of that. He was forced to retire from work to care for his wife, who was fighting cancer – she needed him, and he needed to be with her. I don't think he had planned to actually retire then, but it was just something he had to do, something that love required. He never regretted a minute of it; time spent with the ones you love is never time wasted. In fact, retirement has somewhat mellowed our friend, I don't think he's been in a fight since then. He's had the opportunity to go back to work, full-time or part-time, but he seems content and happy the way things are now...for him, retirement – no matter how it was thrust upon him – has worked out just fine. I'm happy for him.

Dickie just keeps on working...and why not? It keeps him busy, he likes it, he's good at what he does, his company and peers appreciate him and love him and he can put away a little money to help with the college funds of Junior and the unborn (as of this month) grandchild. For Dickie, this is not the right time to retire – he wouldn't be happy with it; he needs to keep on keeping on. Unlike Jerry, who had a bad work schedule Dickie is content with his. He likes what he's doing – he's a valuable employee and he knows it and treats that with respect and loyalty. The question of retirement for Dickie is completely different for him – his needs and issues require an alternative approach – one that fits his lifestyle and plans. We think we may know old Dickie, but it wouldn't surprise me if he has a few hidden agendas and desires he's secretly planning that may end up shocking us all – I hope he does.

I want my little sister to retire NOW. She would love it! Her job is high pressure and tense, and her boss is unreasonable and unpredictable – at this point in her life and career, she doesn't need that crap. Unlike Dickie and his job, Anne's job is hurting her. With our family history of heart problems, she does not need the pressure and tension she currently has – it is not good for her. Her husband knows this, and fully agrees with my opinion; and will support her financially, emotionally and unconditionally – that Marky...he's a good old boy. Anne would have no problem keeping busy and active in retirement... tennis alone would fill the void. But, she has so many other things to accomplish – she still had to finish the book she's working on, she needs to start preparing for grandbabies (I know, I know, but it'll happen...just be patient), she wants to start her own consulting practice, she wants to read more, study more, go to more Royals games (don't we all?), she wants to travel, she wants to visit her brother – Anne Hope – what are you waiting on???? For her, retirement is essential, it is imperative and it is necessary for her to complete her life. And Marky...you know what I'm going to say – you're next!.

As you see, retirement is different for everyone; Conrad retired at age 70, which was perfect for him. And Wandre retired at age 51, which was perfect for her. Larry retired early, Bill never retired and Dickie's still working. We all have to evaluate our lives, our situations in life, our desires and our needs to determine what the right path is for us. I wish Clarence would retire, I wish Susan would re-retire, but mostly I hope everyone does what's ultimately right for them, regardless of what the rest of us think. Except for you Anne Hope! You retire NOW! I MEAN IT!!

17

"Do not try to teach a pig to sing. It wastes your time and annoys the pig."

There's a lot of ugly looking people in the world...that's a bit cruel, but it's true. There are way too many fat people, and I don't care what sort of spin you put on it – fat is not attractive. I go to a gym on a regular basis; I see a lot of the same people there day after day, week after week and year after year. I have never yet seen any person at the gym change his or her body shape or physique. The people who were overweight two years ago are still overweight, people who were flabby three years ago are still flabby; people who were skinny and weak four years ago are still skinny and weak. I just don't see any change in people...I basically think they are what they are. And, one other observation I've made is that most older people are not attractive at all – especially older men – we're just flat out ugly.

I work out. I lift weights, I do cardio – I walk on the treadmill (uphill), I ride the bike, I work out on the elliptical machines and I even do some conditioning classes. It makes me feel really good about myself. I get all pumped up and excited about my workouts. Then, I walk in front of the mirror and wonder who the heck that old guy is. Mirrors can be very depressing...especially in a gym, when you're wearing shorts and maybe a "muscle shirt" (note to my fellow seniors: old guys should never wear muscle shirts – NEVER!).

With all this being said, aren't we glad we're married? How in the world could a bunch of overweight out of shape bald wrinkled sad-looking old dudes like us ever attract a female companion? If you have a wife, you'd better do everything possible to keep her, because trust me old dudes...you are never going to find anyone else to be with your ugly looking self. Women, they're different – they still have an attractiveness and a sexiness when they get older. Us...forget it, we're plain, old, down-and-dirty ugly.

So, guys...stay married. It does you no good whatsoever to try and suck in your stomach when a young girl walks by. That will eventually give you a hernia and temporarily amuse the young lady...it impresses no one. I'm a big fan of marriage – I'd like to go 50-60 years on that bandwagon, at least. Sociologists have reached the conclusion, after many studies, over many years, throughout many different cultures, that "married people" – for whatever reasons – are happier, healthier and better off financially than unmarried people. You can't argue with science.

Being married gives people a reason to work, a home that is usually fairly stable, and children for whom parents feel responsible. And it gives us a regular date...someone to go to movies with, go to dinner with, share with, go to church with, laugh with, someone you can walk around the house in your underwear with, who won't be utterly disgusted with how ugly you are. President Calvin Coolidge was very perceptive when he said this about his wife, "She has endured with my infirmities and I have rejoiced in her graces." Mr. Coolidge may have been a lot things, but he wasn't stupid. Guys, treasure your wives; get down on your knees and thank the good Lord He still allows you to stand next to your lovely wife.

18
"Life is simpler when you plough around the stumps." and "If you have nothing to be grateful for, check your pulse."

And in conclusion…I've determined I'm a cynical, un-trusting person in my older age – not my fault. I've been skewered and lied to and duped and tricked for years now by the media, by our leaders and by our heroes, to the point where I don't really believe anything anymore. That's sad. It should not be that way. I miss the days of Walter Cronkite – you could trust old Walter, at least we thought we could. Our parents could trust President Franklin Roosevelt. Lucy Rutherford who? They could all trust General Eisenhower during WWII. Kay Summersby? Who's that? President George H.W. Bush. "Read my lips…" "I never had sex with that woman…Ms. Lewinsky." Yeah, we know Bill. And Jimmy Swaggart and Jim Bakker would never do the things they did…until they got caught. Who can you trust? Presidents, generals, governors, (certainly not the governor of S.C. who tried to tell us he was hiking the Appalachian Trail, when he was really in South America with his mistress), preachers, teachers – how many of them are in jail now for molesting their students?

I guess it all started for me back in 1963, during those dark, sad days in Dallas, Texas. The FBI and the Secret Service and the news media wanted us then (and still do today) to believe that a janitor in a school book depository was smart enough and a great enough shot to formulate a plan to execute the most powerful man in the world – all by himself. Even when he was arrested and questioned and told them all that he was "just a patsy" in this whole scheme; whoops, he wasn't supposed to say that – let's shut him up quickly. If there's nothing to hide from this sad story, then why are valuable, pertinent documents from the investigation still concealed under lock and key until the year 2017? Huh?

Okay, okay...Enough of the conspiracy stuff...I'm sure no one else had anything to gain from the President's death, it was just a personal vendetta. I get it. I also believe we landed on the moon in 1969. Don't you? I mean, before we went to the moon, NASA had actually orbited men a grand total of 62 miles above the earth's surface. So, what's a mere 225,623 more miles to the moon? Piece of cake. And then, they tell us the spaceship to the moon is travelling at 24,000 MPH, but we're going to slow it down enough to land on the moon's surface without crashing. Then we're going to take off again and come back to earth...okay. Try going 60 mph in your car and stopping suddenly when a deer runs out in front of you. 60 mph! Oh, I'm just messing with you...I believe we went there; heck, I've been to Arizona and Utah and the deserts out west...they don't look anything like the surfaces we saw Neil Armstrong walking on. Cameras can't fake that stuff! No way.

Sports used to be held in high esteem, we could believe Babe Ruth and Ty Cobb and Bill Russell and Bart Starr...men we looked up to and held in high regards. As Paul Simon once wrote, "Where have you gone Joe DiMaggio, our nation turns its lonely eyes to you..." Not anymore. Jolting Joe has left and gone away, and left a bevy of cheaters in his wake. Baseball's most sacred record – 61 home runs in a season. Smashed by a slew of steroidal, cheating bums. We all should have been outraged when a skinny player for the Baltimore Orioles named Brady Anderson hit 52 home runs one year – when the most he'd ever hit before in his life was 12. But we just overlooked it. No one thought anything was weird when Sammy Sosa and Mark McGuire started hitting more home runs that anyone had in nearly 40 years. Everyone thought Barry Bonds had just improved...did anyone bother to look at "before" and "after" pictures of Mr. Bonds? Well, they all eventually were caught and exposed...America, we've been lied to again.

Heck, we even believed Lance Armstrong was clean while he was winning 7 consecutive Tours de France...I mean, he said he was clean. And he was from Texas and he'd beaten cancer, and he was a good old boy – he wouldn't lie to us. Right. After Lance was exposed, the officials of the Tour thought about giving his winning trophy to the guy who finished behind Lance, who hadn't doped and cheated. They nixed that idea when it was determined that the champion would have been the guy who finished in 23rd place!

Bob Dylan, poor old guy, can't sing a lick...I mean he can't sing a lick; however, he does try. Unlike Brittany or Madonna, or (fill in the blanks), untold others who try to fool us by lip-synching. Why should cheating be limited to politics or sports, heck, let's lip-synch too – who'll ever know? Who will ever know that our college sports heroes are not writing their own papers in school – I believe it! Heck, I even believe it when people come up to me in the gym and say, "Hey old dude, you're really looking good!" And finally, I really believed it when my girlfriend broke up with me after my freshman year in college when she told me, "It's not you...it's me."